wise words
politics, business
small talk

Deborah Capras

Cover: loopgrafikdesign

ISBN: 978-3-946091-01-1

CONTENTS

It's not taboo — it's interesting!

'Man is by nature a political animal.'

Aristotle (384–322BC)
Greek philosopher

'Der Mensch ist von Natur aus ein politisches Tier.'

Generally, business people enjoy making small talk as much as everyone else! It can be fun and good for business. Small talk can help you understand your business partners and the culture in which they do business — it helps you learn what makes them tick.

But if all you talk about is the weather, small talk can get very boring pretty quickly. And despite what you may have heard, there aren't really many topics that are truly taboo. You've heard that politics is taboo? Nonsense. Politics are a part of life and an important part of business. You can't ignore politics when you do business internationally.

Five tips
Basically, you need to remember these five tips when you make small talk — on politics or any other topic:

1. Show respect.
2. Show interest.
3. Share what you know.
4. Find a personal connection.
5. Don't criticize.

How to learn vocabulary

To make interesting small talk, you'll need some interesting words. In this book, you'll find key words, word partnerships, phrases and idioms that you will need to talk about politics.

Business and politics are similar in many ways. That's why you will also hear 'political' expressions at work. We provide you with the best ones here, too.

From five to 50 in five!

You need time to learn vocabulary. Most brains can only remember five things at a time. If you can learn five things well, you can move them into your long-term memory.

In this book, there are five sections. In each section, you will find five key political terms and five idiomatic expressions for business situations, which makes a total of 50 vocabulary items.

Spend five minutes on each word, translation, definition and example sentence — in no time you'll have 50 expressions that you can use to talk about politics and your business.

Checklist of five steps

1. Check your understanding
Read the explanation and example sentence. Check the translation.

2. Spell it correctly
Close your eyes and spell the word or expression in your head.

3. Use it in your own sentence
First, create sentences in your head — then write them down.

4. Take a break
Close the book and think about something else for five seconds. Before you open the book again, try to remember the word and the definition, or the word and the translation, or one example sentence. Repeat these steps five times and then take a break for five minutes.

5. Get active.
Read the small talk fact file and do the activity at the end of the section.

1 THE VOTE

'If voting changed anything, they'd abolish it.'

Ken Livingston (1945–)
British politician (1987–2001) and former mayor
of London (2000–2008)

'Wenn wählen etwas ändern würde, würden sie es abschaffen.'

1. vote (against/for sb./sth.)
In politics, you vote for a party, a person, an idea or an ideology.

- 'We vote for a new government every five years.'

In business, when you make a formal choice for or against someone or something, especially in a meeting, you can also use 'vote'.

- 'I vote for a coffee break right now. What about you?'

German: wählen; gegen/für jdn./etw. stimmen

2. vote
In politics, if you have the vote, you can help decide who will be a member of parliament, or MP, and therefore who will form a government. You can 'cast a vote'.

- 'Everyone over 18 has the vote — and every vote counts.'

In business, every vote counts, too. It's common to say 'take a vote' or 'hold a vote'.

- 'Let's decide this together. Let's take a vote now.'

German: Stimme, Abstimmung; abstimmen

3. vote of (no) confidence

In politics, a vote of confidence can make or break a government, a party or a politician. One example is when all the people in parliament vote on whether they support the prime minister or not.

- 'The prime minister won the vote of confidence by just two votes.'

In business, we can use the same expression to show that someone in a senior position in a company has — or does not have — support.

- 'The manager suffered a vote of no confidence when his team refused to work on the project.'

German: (Miss-)Vertrauensvotum

4. poll

In politics, we talk a lot about polls. The polls are the places where people vote. We also call them 'polling stations'. When we ask people about how they voted when they leave the polling station, we take an 'exit poll'. During an election, the country 'goes to the polls'.

- 'In the UK, the polls close at 10 p.m.'

In business, we talk about polls, too, but especially about 'opinion polls'. These are assessments of how people feel about specific things. 'Poll' can be used as a noun and a verb. You poll people to get information for your opinion polls.

- 'We need to arrange some opinion polls to find out what people think about the new designs.'

German: Wahllokale; Umfrage; jdn. befragen

5. eligible
In politics, if you are eligible to vote, you have the right to vote. You can vote.

- 'If you are a British citizen but have lived abroad for more than 15 years, you are no longer eligible to vote in the UK.'

In business, if you are eligible for something or to do something, you have the right to have or do it.

- 'Employees who are eligible for the bonus will receive payment at the end of the month.'

German: zu etw. berechtigt sein

Key 'vote' idiomatic expressions for business

1. like turkeys voting for Christmas
In many English-speaking countries, Turkeys are traditionally eaten at Christmas. So, it makes sense that if turkeys had the choice, they wouldn't vote for Christmas. We use this expression to show that a decision or option would make a situation worse.

- 'I can't agree to move the offices to a place where nobody wants to live. That would be like turkeys voting for Christmas.'

German: das ist, als würden die Gänse für Weihnachten stimmen

2. deciding vote
The deciding vote is the most important one. It's also called the casting vote.

- 'John, it's five-five. You're the last one, so you have the deciding vote. What's it to be?'

German: die ausschlaggebende Stimme

3. sb./sth. gets my vote

If somebody or something gets your vote, then you support that person or thing. It doesn't necessarily mean that you are able to vote for that person or thing in an official way.

- 'He definitely gets my vote. Just listen to the way he talks.'

German: er/es kriegt meine Stimme

4. put sth. to the vote

When you put something to the vote, you ask people whether they are for or against something.

- 'I think it's a good idea to work on Saturday, but I'm not sure if the team will feel the same way. Let's put it to the vote.'

German: über etw. abstimmen lassen

5. vote with your feet

If you don't like something, you don't buy it or you don't go there. You show what you think of it by using — or not using — your feet: you vote with your feet.

- 'When they found out that the restaurant didn't use fresh vegetables and fruit, people voted with their feet. It closed after a month.'

German: mit den Füssen abstimmen

Small talk fact file: the vote
It's not a good idea to ask someone directly about the person or party that they voted for. It's really none of your business! But what if elections are taking place in your business partner's country? Do you still not talk about them? If you don't ask, does that make you look better or worse in the eyes of your partner? You decide!

If you're interested in politics and you know your business partner well, you could ask about the voting system.

Here's a small talk fact file from the UK:
The general election is the most important one in the UK. It's the election where we vote for the prime minister. This kind of election is always on a Thursday. Do you know why? No? Don't worry — the British don't either!

There are many possible reasons, but this is the one that I like. When people vote on Thursday, we know who has won the election by Friday. Over the weekend, the old government can move out and the new government can move in — and start work on Monday. (If the old government wins, it can celebrate over the weekend!)

It's possible to have an election on another day, but the last time this happened was on Tuesday, 27 October 1931.

Checklist of five steps

1. Check your understanding
2. Spell it correctly
3. Use it in your own sentence
4. Take a break
5. Get active!

What small talk facts about voting in your country — or in any other countries — would you be happy to share and discuss with a business partner?

- Write down one fact.
- Turn it into a story.
- Record it.
- Listen to it.
- Reflect on it.
- Improve it.
- You're ready to go!

2 THE PARTY

'Power tends to corrupt and
absolute power corrupts
absolutely.'

Lord Acton (1834–1902)
British historian

'Macht korrumpiert, absolute Macht korrumpiert absolut.'

1. party

In politics, a party is a group of people who have similar political ideas and feelings. Political parties can be centrist, left-wing or right-wing — and they can be fascist, green, independent, populist, progressive, radical, revolutionary and social democratic, too. The party in power is the party that governs the country. The parties that are not in power, are the parties in opposition.

- 'How many major parties are there in the UK?'

In business, a 'party' can be a person, a group of people or an organisation that you are doing business with — or are in a dispute with.

- 'Both parties agree to stop using the logo on their websites.'

German: Vertragspartei; Seite; Partei

2. fringe

In politics, a fringe group or party is one that has opinions that are very different to the rest of society.

- 'Nobody takes him seriously. He belongs to a fringe group in the opposition.'

In business, you will see 'fringe' used mostly together with 'benefit'. If you work for a travel company, for example, you may get cheap flights. This is a 'fringe benefit', something that is extra to your normal payment.

- 'What are the best fringe benefits that I have in this job? The car — and the free lunches.'

German: Rand; fringe benefit: freiwillige Lohnnebenleistungen

3. mainstream

In politics, the major parties are the mainstream parties. They usually focus on mainstream politics, such as health, education and the economy. This is because they look after the mainstream — the people or things that are viewed as normal or ordinary by most people in society.

- 'In the UK, only the mainstream parties have a chance at choosing a prime minister.'

In business, you can use 'mainstream' to talk about ordinary things, especially in marketing.

- 'The music is very mainstream. It's perfect for our teenager customers.'

German: Mainstream, Hauptrichtung, alltäglich

4. chair

In politics, the party chair is the person who leads the party. We also say chairperson/chairman or chairwoman.

- 'The party chair called on its members to support the initiative.'

In business, we talk about the chairman or chairwoman of a company. In everyday business, we refer to the person who leads a meeting as the chair. That person chairs the meeting.

- 'OK, so I'll chair the meeting today. Let's get started.'

German: Parteivorsitzende; chairman/woman = Vorstandvorsitzende, Vorsitzende; den Vorsitz haben

5. grassroots

In politics, anything that is described as 'grassroots' is started and led by the people, not by the established parties or politicians. Political parties use the expression when they want to look more 'connected' to the people.

- 'This is a grassroots campaign. We're working with the people and for the people.'

In business, you will hear about 'grassroots' in marketing and advertising most. If a company organises a grassroots marketing campaign, it will try to get very close to its customers during the campaign — and will try to get its customers to interact with the campaign. This is also viral marketing and word-of-mouth marketing. It makes use of the people who use the products or services to advertise to other people, usually friends. It's become easier with social media.

- 'Grassroots marketing can be very powerful. If you hear from your best friend via Twitter that a product is good, you will believe it!'

German: Basisbewegung (eine Initiative, die von der Bevölkerung gestartet wird); Mundpropaganda

Key 'party' expressions for business

1. toe the party line

The expression 'toe the party line' comes from sports. In a race, you have to stand with your toes behind the line — you should not go over it. If you go over the line before you should, you will have problems. When politicians 'toe the party line', they do what the leader of the party wants them to do — which may not always be what they really want to do. In business, you can use the same expression to show that people are doing what management wants.

- 'I don't find it difficult to toe the party line — I think the company has the right vision and will have a great future.'

German: sich der Parteilinie unterwerfen; sich anpassen

2. no tea party

In the US, the tea party is a political right-wing movement that started in 2009, but this party has nothing to do with the idiom 'no tea party'. We use this expression to show that something is difficult. A real tea party, with cakes, sandwiches and tea is, in comparison, relatively easy to organise.

- 'We know it'll be no tea party, but we're planning to open a shop in London this year.'

German: kein Kinderspiel

3. be a party to sth.

If you are party to something, you know about it and are involved in it. We sometimes use this expression to show that someone was party to something illegal, unethical or wrong. We use the expression 'I wasn't a party to something' to show that we were not part of something or have no idea of the details.

- I wasn't party to the deal with the company so I have no idea when we will start working together.'

German: etw. von einer Abmachung wissen; in ein Geheimnis eingeweiht sein, an einem Verbrechen beteiligt sein

4. have a hidden agenda

Political parties always have an agenda, and they sometimes have a hidden agenda, too. An agenda is a plan. If you have a hidden agenda, you have a reason for doing something that you don't tell people about — you keep your real reason for doing it a secret. Most commonly in business, an agenda is the plan for a meeting.

- 'I don't have a hidden agenda. I only want to know how much the program costs. Honestly, I'm not saying it's too expensive.'

German: geheime Pläne haben; Hintergedanken; Tagesordnung

5. open-door policy

When a party has an 'open-door policy', it believes that people and products should be able to enter the country freely. At work, when someone has an open door policy, that person is happy for other people to come into the office at any time to ask questions.

- 'If you have any questions, come and see me in my office at any time. In this company, we believe in an open-door policy.'

German: Politik der offenen Tür; immer zu sprechen sein

Small talk fact file: the party
For a country to be democratic, it needs more than one party. You can find out about the culture of a country by learning about the most popular parties — and not just about the party that is in power.

Here's a small talk fact file from the UK:
Britain seems to be a multi-party system. However, at the election in 2015, Britain really only had three mainstream parties: Labour, the Conservatives and the Scottish National Party. Other smaller parties in parliament include UKIP, a populist party which is much more right-wing than the Conservatives, and the Green Party, which won one seat for the first time in 2010! The Liberal Democrats formed a government with the Conservatives in 2010, but in the 2015 elections they lost many votes and the Conservatives were able to form a government without them.

At every election, there are always a couple of fringe parties, some of which have crazy names — and crazy agendas. The most famous is probably the 'Monster Raving Loony Party'. I'm not joking.

Checklist of five steps

1. Check your understanding
2. Spell it correctly
3. Use it in your own sentence
4. Take a break
5. Get active!

What small talk facts about the parties in your country — or in any other countries — would you be happy to share and discuss with a business partner?

- Write down one fact.
- Turn it into a story.
- Record it.
- Listen to it.
- Reflect on it.
- Improve it.
- You're ready to go!

2 THE PEOPLE

'No woman in my time will be prime minister'.

Margaret Thatcher (1925–2013), spoken in 1969.

Former British prime minister (1979–90)

'Ich glaube nicht, dass es zu meinen Lebzeiten einen weiblichen Premierminister geben wird.'

1. pundit

In politics, this is an analyst, commentator, or writer who usually works for a newspaper or magazine, or in TV/radio. It comes from a Sanskrit phrase meaning 'the learned one'.

- 'So, it seems that the pundits can't agree on who will win the next election. Well, that's no surprise.'

In business, we can also use this word to talk about experts.

- 'Pundits are saying that we will see more wearable apps in the business world in the future — and not just for fitness.'

German: Experte/Expertin

2. candidate

In politics, a candidate is a person who is nominated for election.

- 'The Green party candidate wants to create a no-cars zone in the city centre.'

In business, a candidate is a person who applies for a job.

- 'We have a number of strong candidates, but I think Carol is the best.'

German: Kandidat(in); Bewerber(in)

3. secretary
In politics, a secretary can be someone with a very important position, such as the foreign secretary. In the US, this it the Secretary of State. Most political parties also have a press secretary.

- 'We have never had a female secretary of defence.'

In business, we also have secretaries, but they are often called Pas, or personal assistants.

- 'My secretary will contact you about the meeting.'

German: Minister(in); Außenminister(in);
Verteidigungsminister(in); Pressesprecher(in); (Chef)sekretärin

4. shadow minister
In politics, shadow ministers belong to the shadow cabinet. They are not in power, but in opposition.

- 'The shadow ministers can be very critical, but if they were in power, they would probably make the same mistakes.'

In business, we talk about the shadow economy, instead of shadow ministers. This is illegal business. At work, on a more general level, we use the verb 'shadow'. When you start at a new company, you might 'shadow' someone who has worked at the company for longer, so that you can learn how people do things.

- 'You will shadow someone for the first week, so you get an idea of how things work here.'

German: Schattenminister(in); Schattenwirtschaft; jmdn auf Schritt und Tritt begleiten

5. supporter
In politics, a supporter is someone who agrees with a particular party and votes for that party.

- 'Politicians like to be near their supporters for photographs.'

In business, we rarely talk about 'supporters' at work, but we do use the noun 'support' and the verb 'support' regularly. If you support something, you like it, approve it and want it to happen. You have someone's support.

- 'We have the support of the whole team. We really expect this idea to be a success.'

German: Anhänger(in); jmdn. etw. unterstützen; etw. befürworten

Key 'political people' expressions for business

1. dark horse

In horse racing, a dark horse is a horse that wins unexpectedly — it's a horse that nobody believed would win. And nobody put money on it to win. We say someone is a dark horse if that person wins something unexpectedly, also in politics. In business, we also use it to describe someone who has a secret skill or talent that surprises everyone when they find out about it.

- 'I never knew you could play the piano. You're a bit of a dark horse, aren't you?'

German: unbekannte Größe; unbeschriebenes Blatt

2. spin doctor

In politics, if you want to control the story, you need a spin doctor. This is a negative expression for the press secretary. In business, sometimes you will need to change information a little to make it sound more positive than it really is: you put a spin, or even a positive spin, on it. It happens all the time in politics.

- 'It's not easy, but how can we put a positive spin on this?'

German: Pressesprecher(in); etw. ins rechte Licht rücken

3. lame duck

Politicians, and especially presidents, are called lame ducks when they are not very powerful. A lame duck is a duck that is hurt and not able to walk well. In business, it's someone who is not very successful.

- 'He's a bit of a lame duck as a manager.'

German: Niete; ineffektive Person

4. front runner

The front runner is the best person and the person who is certain to win — an election, race, competition or even a job application.

- 'Do we have a front runner for the job?'

German: Spitzenreiter(in)

5. public figure

Politicians are public figures — they are in the public eye.

- 'He's a public figure so he has to accept that there will be a lot of interest in where he spends his holidays — at least there will be in the UK.'

German: Figur des öffentlichen Lebens

Small talk fact file: the people
How do people feel about the people in politics in
your country?

Here's one a small talk fact file from the UK:
It's true that people have become very cynical about
politics in the UK. People find it hard to believe what
politicians say. We don't believe their promises — and
we don't believe their statistics, either. We expect
politicians to lie — or at least not to tell the whole
truth. We know they have spin doctors to make them
look good in the media. Politicians don't always know
how to use social media themselves. In the UK, we've
had a number of scandals when politicians say the
craziest things on Twitter. Actually, they often say
what they are really thinking on Twitter. Maybe it's
crazy that they lose their jobs for this reason!

Checklist of five steps

1. Check your understanding
2. Spell it correctly
3. Use it in your own sentence
4. Take a break
5. Get active!

What small talk facts about some key public figures in politics in your country — or in any other countries — would you be happy to share and discuss with a business partner?

* Write down one fact.
* Turn it into a story.
* Record it.
* Listen to it.
* Reflect on it.
* Improve it.
* You're ready to go!

4 THE SYSTEM

'A day like today is not a day for sound bites... but I feel the hand of history upon our shoulder.'

Tony Blair (1953–)
Former British prime minister (1997–2007)

April 1998, shortly before the Good Friday
agreement, which led to peace in Northern Ireland
and an end to the Troubles.

*'Ein Tag wie dieser ist nicht ein Tag für markante Sprüche...
aber ich spüre die Hand der Geschichte auf unserer. Schulter.'*

1. first-past-the-post

In politics, this is the system that is used in the UK. It comes from horse racing — the first horse to go past the post, or line, is the winner. In this type of political system, voters can only vote for one candidate and the candidate who gets the most votes becomes a member of parliament (MP).

- 'Some people are critical of the first-past-the-post system. They would prefer proportional representation as they have in Germany.'

In business, most votes are based on a kind of 'first-past-the-post' system, but we don't normally use this expression to talk about it. More important 'posts' are the job kind. These are usually filled not by votes, but by a careful selection process.

- 'We hope to fill the post by the end of the month.'

German: Mehrheitswahlrecht; Stelle

2. the establishment

In politics, particularly in the UK, the establishment is a mix of the traditions, institutions and powerful people in society, including politicians.

- 'The queen is part of the establishment, just as much as the politicians.'

In business, we don't use 'the establishment' in the same way. As a noun, it's a very formal way to refer to a business ('a family establishment'). We do use the verb 'establish' in many different situations at work. Basically, it means 'make something exist or happen'.

- 'My father established the business in 1975.'

German: das Establishment (die politisch einflussreichen Kreise); Organisation; etw. *schaffen, herstellen, gründen, aufstellen u.s.w.*

3. issue

In politics, it's important to focus on the big issues, such as the economy, education and housing.

- 'Everyone was talking about the big issues, but Labour focused on TV debates.'

In business, we often focus on issues. They are important problems or difficult situations.

- 'There are still some issues with the design. The colour isn't right.'

German: wichtiges / zentrales Thema; Problem; Frage

4. seat

In politics, if you have a seat, you have received enough votes to win a place in parliament. You can also have a seat on a committee or other institutions.

- 'The party lost most of its seats in the election.'

In business, you will hear 'seat' in many different situations. From the first 'take a seat' when you meet people, to 'be in the driving seat' or 'take a back seat' when you have meetings with them. They are all common expressions in business.

- 'I'll take a back seat in the next meeting. You should ask all the questions.'

German: Sitz; Platz nehmen; die Zügel in der Hand haben; in den Hintergrund treten

5. constitution

In politics, the constitution refers to the basic laws and principles that decide how a country is governed. From the same word family, we have the constituents (the people who vote), and the constituency (the specific area where certain constituents vote).

- 'The UK doesn't have a written constitution, did you know that?'

In business, companies have constitutions, too. These are the rules that decide how the company is governed.

- 'His actions were not allowed under the constitution. That's why he lost his job.'

German: Verfassung; Grundgesetz; Wähler; Wahlbezirk; Satzung (der Gesellschaft)

Key 'system' expressions for business

1. quid pro quo
This is Latin for 'something for something'. In business, just as in politics, people often expect something for doing something.

- 'There's a lot of quid pro quo in networking. The more you share and help people, the more you get out of your contacts.'

German: Gegenleistung

2. sound bite
Politics are all about sound bites now. These are simply short, interesting things that people say. Politicians are sometimes criticized for talking only in sound bites. They know that the short statements will be quoted in the media — or on Twitter and other social media. In business, it's sometimes useful to be able to describe your ideas in sound bites, too.

- 'Can you describe what your company does in a sound bite? You should be able to.'

German: markanter Spruch

3. blink first
Negotiations are an important part of politics and business. In both, it's often a question of who will blink first. The person who blinks first, loses.

- 'I expect them to blink first. They need us as an investor or they're finished.'

German: zuerst blinzeln; nachgeben

4. kick the can down the road
Kicking the can down the road is what politicians sometimes do best. It means that they avoid doing something about the problem. The expression is also used in business.

- 'Let's not kick the can down the road any longer. It's time to make a decision about Rodney.'

German: ein Problem vor sich schieben

5. vested interest
When politicians have a vested interest in something, they have a personal reason for acting the way they do — usually because they will get a financial benefit from it. Business is no different. It often works along the same system.

- 'The problem is, Brian has a vested interest in giving the contract to that company. His brother works there.'

German: an etw. ein starkes persönliches Interesse haben

Small talk fact file: the system
Plato, the Classical Greek philosopher, described five types of systems — or regimes: aristocracy, timocracy, oligarchy, democracy and tyranny.

Although most people describe Ancient Greece as having a democracy, its regime was more like a timocracy, which is when people who own property are in charge.

Here's a small talk fact file from the UK:
Have you heard about the old boy network? In the UK, this is how we describe a group of people who help each other. The people in the group are usually men (that's why it's an 'old boy' network and not 'old girl') who all went to the same school or university, such as Oxford or Cambridge, who know the same people and who, most importantly, use their power or position to help other people in the group. It's a system that helps people to get jobs, positions and to get votes.

Checklist of five steps

1. Check your understanding
2. Spell it correctly
3. Use it in your own sentence
4. Take a break
5. Get active!

What small talk facts about the political system in your country — or in any other countries — would you be happy to share and discuss with a business partner?

- Write down one fact.
- Turn it into a story.
- Record it.
- Listen to it.
- Reflect on it.
- Improve it.
- You're ready to go!

4 THE RESULTS

'I believe there is something out there watching us. Unfortunately, it's the government.'

Woody Allen (1935–)
American film director, writer and actor

'Ich glaube, es gibt etwas, da draussen, das uns beobachtet.
Leider ist es die Regierung.'

1. landslide victory

In politics, if the election ends with a landslide victory, then there is one clear winner who has received a lot more votes than every other party.

- 'There were no surprises. It was a landslide victory again.'

In business, you might hear about a Pyrrhic victory — this is a victory that is not worth winning, as you have to lose too much to win it. The term is named after the Greek King Pyrrhus of Epirus. In 280 BC, he won an important victory over the Romans, but he lost many important men in the battle.

- 'I told him it was a Pyrrhic victory at best. We may have won the contract, but we won't make any money on the deal.'

German: Pyrrhussieg

2. hung parliament

In politics, this is an election result in which no party has enough seats to form a government on its own.

- 'A hung parliament would mean at least ten days without a government.'

In business, we don't have 'hung parliaments', but we do have 'hung juries' in law. This is when the jury cannot agree on whether someone is guilty or not guilty.

- 'The fraud trial ended in a hung jury. There will be another court case in June.'

German: Parlament ohne klare Mehrheitsverhältnisse, Jury, die zu keinem Mehrheitsurteil kommt

3. absolute majority
In politics, parties want an absolute majority after an election. If they don't have an absolute majority, the party with the most votes can try to form a coalition with another party or parties.

- 'As no party has the absolute majority, the two main parties will form a coalition.'

In business, it's rare that we talk about absolute majorities, but we do like to talk about who has a 'majority interest' in a company. This is the person, or organization, that has more than half of all the shares in the company. It's also called a 'controlling interest'.

- 'They have a majority interest in the company so of course they can decide what happens to the factory.'

German: absolute Mehrheit; Mehrheitsbesitz

4. minority government
In politics, a minority government is a government in which the ruling party has less the half the total of the seats in parliament. It's rare to find a minority government, especially one that can last.

- 'As neither party has the absolute majority, and neither wants to form a coalition with any other party, the only option is a minority government. Or new elections.'

In business, we don't talk about minority governments, but we do talk about who has a 'minority interest' in a company. This is when someone owns some shares in a company, but not enough to control what happens to the company.

- 'We're looking to sell a minority interest in our start-up.'

German: Fremdanteil; Minderheitsanteil

5. do a U-turn
In politics, many parties do a U-turn after winning. They just can't keep their election promises.

- 'I knew it. They did a U-turn on their education plan in their first week in office.'

In business, you sometimes hear about U-turns when talking about dramatic changes in plans or strategies. It's also a useful expression if you drive. You do, or make, a U-turn when you turn your car in the shape of a U, so that you can go back in the direction where you came from. Just make sure you don't do any illegal U-turns.

- 'Keep driving and do a U-turn at the end of this road.'

German: eine Kehrtwendung machen; wenden

Key 'results' expressions for business

1. neck-and-neck
When competitors in a race are neck and neck, they are very close. In business, it's rare to have a neck-and-neck race. But you will hear other 'neck' expressions. You'll hear 'pain in the neck' to describe someone who is very annoying. A nice expression for small talk is 'neck of the woods'. It means 'a particular area'.

- 'So, what's happening in your neck of the woods?'

German: Kopf-an-Kopf; ein Dorn im Auge; ein Nervensäge; in diesen/jds. Breiten

2. a win-win situation
In politics, and in business, everyone likes to say that they can offer a win-win situation. This is a situation when everyone benefits.

- 'Believe me, this is a win-win situation for us all.'

German: eine Situation, in der man nur gewinnen kann

3. crunch time

An election is an important period of time when a decision is finally made. It's a critical situation and that's why we call it 'crunch time'. We use the expression to say that it's time to make an important decision.

In business, this is usually just before an important deadline.

- 'The customers are coming tomorrow and they will want to see a design. It's crunch time!'

German: entscheidende Phase

4. throw in the towel

When you throw in the towel, you give up. The expression comes from boxing.

- 'I can understand why you would want to throw in the towel right now, but I think you should keep trying.'

German: das Handtuch werfen

5. make the cut

After the election, some politicians will make the cut, others won't. If you don't make the cut, you're not chosen. This expression is used when we want to show that the reason why someone wasn't chosen is because they weren't good enough. We can use this expression in business to say that someone has, or hasn't, been chosen for something, especially for a job.

- 'I thought I had a good chance, but I didn't make the cut.'

German: erfolgreich sein

Small talk fact file: the results
The results are the most important part of an election. However, the last thing you should do in business is criticize the winner of an election in another culture. You can explore how your business partners might feel about the results by keeping the conversation very general.

Here's a small talk fact file from the UK:
What will the election results mean for business? It's usually hard to say. The winning party has often made a lot of promises, but they rarely keep them. I always expect them to do a U-turn on at least a couple of their promises.

In the UK, one of the most important events on the political calendar is the budget. This is when the finance minister, or as we call him the chancellor of the exchequer, says how much money the country has, and how the government plans to save and spend money over the next year. Most people just listen to find out if they will have to pay more or less tax.
The budget usually takes place in March or April, just before the elections in May, if there is one in that year. This means that if the winning party is a different party, they will have to live with the budget from the previous government. The winner may not feel that they have really won!

Checklist of five steps

1. Check your understanding
2. Spell it correctly
3. Use it in your own sentence
4. Take a break
5. Get active!

What small talk facts about the election results in your country — or in any other countries — would you be happy to share and discuss with a business partner?

- Write down one fact.
- Turn it into a story.
- Record it.
- Listen to it.
- Reflect on it.
- Improve it.
- You're ready to go!

A FINAL TEST

Well done! You've reached the final chapter! This is where we test whether this book of *wise words* has helped you improve your vocabulary.

We have 20 questions on the expressions in *wise words*. You'll find the answers on page 59.

1. 'The manager suffered a vote of no _____ when his team refused to work on the project.'

2. 'We need to arrange some opinion _____ to find out what people think about the new designs.'

3. 'I can't agree to move the offices to a place where nobody wants to live. That would be like _____ voting for Christmas.'

4. 'I think it's a good idea to work on Saturday, but I'm not sure if the team will feel the same way. Let's _____ it to the vote.'

5. 'What are the best _____ benefits that I have in this job? The car — and the free lunches.'

6. 'OK, so I'll _____ the meeting today. Let's get started.'

7. 'I don't find it difficult to _____ the party line — I think the company has the right vision and will have a great future.'

8. 'I don't have a _____ agenda. I only want to know how much the program costs. I'm not saying it's too expensive.'

9. '_____ are saying that we will see more wearable apps in the business world in the future — and not just for fitness.'

10. 'We have a number of strong _____, but I think Carol is the best.'

11. 'It's not easy, but how can we put a positive _____ on this?'

12. 'He's a _____ figure so he has to accept that there will be a lot of interest in where he spends his holidays — at least there will be in the UK.'

13. 'We hope to fill the _____ by the end of the month.'

14. 'There are still some _____ with the design. The colour isn't right.'

15. 'I'll take a back _____ in the next meeting. You should ask all the questions.'

16. 'Can you describe what your company does in a sound _____? You should be able to.'

17. 'Let's not kick the _____ down the road any longer. It's time to make a decision about Rodney.'

18. 'They have a majority _____ in the company so of course they can decide what happens to the factory.'

19. 'Keep driving and do a _____ at the end of this road.'

20. 'The customers are coming tomorrow and they will want to see a design. It's _____ time!'

Answers

1. confidence

'The manager suffered **a vote of no confidence** when his team refused to work on the project.'

German: (Miss-)Vertrauensvotum

2. polls

'We need to arrange some **opinion polls** to find out what people think about the new designs.'

German: Umfrage

3. turkeys

'I can't agree to move the offices to a place where nobody wants to live. That would be **like turkeys voting for Christmas**.'

German: das ist, als würden die Gänse für Weihnachten stimmen

4. put

'I think it's a good idea to work on Saturday, but I'm not sure if the team will feel the same way. Let's **put it to the vote**.'

German: über etw. abstimmen lassen

5. fringe

'What are the best **fringe benefits** that I have in this job? The car — and the free lunches.'
German: Rand; fringe benefit: freiwillige Lohnnebenleistungen

6. chair

'OK, so I'll **chair** the meeting today. Let's get started.'
German: den Vorsitz haben

7. toe

'I don't find it difficult to **toe the party line** — I think the company has the right vision and will have a great future.'
German: sich der Parteilinie unterwerfen; sich anpassen

8. have a hidden agenda

'I don't have a **hidden agenda**. I only want to know how much the program costs. I'm not saying it's too expensive.'
German: geheime Pläne haben; Hintergedanken; Tagesordnung

9. pundit

'**Pundits** are saying that we will see more wearable apps in the business world in the future — and not just for fitness.'
German: Experte/Expertin

10. **candidate**

'We have a number of strong **candidates**, but I think Carol is the best.'
German: Bewerber(in)

11. **spin**

'It's not easy, but how can we **put a positive spin on** this?'
German: etw. ins rechte Licht rücken

12. **public**

'He's a **public figure** so he has to accept that there will be a lot of interest in where he spends his holidays — at least there will be in the UK.'
German: Figur des öffentlichen Lebens

13. **post**

'We hope to fill the **post** by the end of the month.'
German: Stelle

14. **issues**

'There are still some **issues** with the design. The colour isn't right.'
German: Problem

15. seat

'I'll **take a back seat** in the next meeting. You should ask all the questions.'
German: in den Hintergrund treten

16. bite

'Can you describe what your company does in a **sound bite**? You should be able to.'
German: markanter Spruch

17. can

'Let's not **kick the can down the road** any longer. It's time to make a decision about Rodney.'
German: ein Problem vor sich schieben

18. interest

'They have a **majority interest** in the company so of course they can decide what happens to the factory.'
German: Mehrheitsbesitz

19. U-turn

'Keep driving and **do a U-turn** at the end of this road.'
German: wenden

20. crunch

'The customers are coming tomorrow and they will want to see a design. It's **crunch time**!'
German: entscheidende Phase

ABOUT THE AUTHOR

Deborah Capras is an experienced and respected business English author, editor, trainer and teacher trainer. She has written for *Business Spotlight*, Germany's leading magazine for learners of business English, since its launch in 2001 and was the deputy editor of the magazine from 2009 until 2015. She has developed a successful range of print, audio and digital language-learning products, in particular for the business English market and for in-company trainings.

Deborah delivers language and management training workshops, seminars and webinars and gives talks and presentations on the topic of language acquisition, the use of technology in language-learning and publishing. She has a background in linguistics and pedagogy, as well as extensive experience of management issues and production processes.

More wise words!

Don't miss out on wise words. We'll be publishing more vocabulary wise words on other topics on a regular basis. Sign up for our newsletter and we'll let you know when they are on sale.

Sign up for the wise words newsletter at

http://eepurl.com/buj7o1

Have you got a request, comment or criticism? Send us an email and we'll look into it:

deborahcapras@wise-words.com
www.wise-words.com

www.ingramcontent.com/pod-product-compliance
Lightning Source LLC
Chambersburg PA
CBHW032307210326
41520CB00047B/2272